KID
MOMENTS
Poetry for Early Readers

DEBORAH ANN MARTIN

Illustrations By Her Grandchildren

Kid Moments - Poetry for Early Readers
Part of the Life Moments Series

By Deborah Ann Martin
Illustrations By Her Grandchildren

ISBN:
eBook: 978-1-966771-28-9
Soft: 978-1-966771-29-6
Hard: 978-1-966771-30-2

www. Survivinglifelessons.com

This book is dedicated to my grandchildren.

Table of Contents

Giggle Time

"Having fun with children creates connection. Connection builds relationships. Relationships are what we need to raise our children. So start having more fun, more of the time" – Bridget Miller

Clowns

Clowns,

Dressed in

Big red shoes

Painted faces,

Bright, colorful clothes and a big red nose,

Make children smile by giving a balloon.

Some do magic

Ride animals,

Or give

Candy.

Some

Funny

Clowns will ride

Unicycles.

Clowns make the world a nicer place to be.

Silly Little Girl

I am a silly little girl

Who likes to dance and whirl

To happily sing aloud

In front of any crowd

And when I'm finished with my song

I skip merrily along.

The Ball

A ball

A ball

A bouncy ball

You throw it up

And see it fall.

The sky

The sky

The pretty sky

The ball falls down

And bounces high

Noses

Why do all kids pick their noses and eat it?

Runny or Not,

It's still snot.

Why eat

Snot?

Oreos

i have eaten

the oreos

that was in

the cupboard

i know you

set aside

for your snack

forgive me

i was so

much fun pulling

it apart and

eating the

creamy white

filling then

dipping the

cookie in

a nice cold

glass of milk

Silly

Lily was silly

When she rolled

Down the hilly

With Billy.

Blackbeard

A Blackbeard pirate I want to be.

I want to sail the "Murky" seas.

I want to travel far and away.

It would be fun to hunt for treasures each day.

Pirates love to laugh and sing.

Through the fog, you would hear their laughter ring.

There are many countries I would like to see.

A Blackbeard pirate is what I want to be.

I would wear a patch to look a little mean.

A proud walk and a growl are what I would need.

I would climb the tallest sail.

In ports, I would speak of pirate tales.

There are so many adventures for me.

I cannot wait to sail the seven seas.

Benjamin Harry

Benjamin Harry

Made a face that was scary.

In the water, he saw his reflection

Then took off in the opposite direction.

Silly Me

Silly ol' me.

How can it be?

I laughed so hard.

I had to pee.

Andy

My friend Andy

Couldn't eat candy.

Not having anything sweet

Made him have sour feet.

Dragon

Aiden loves to play pretend
A dragon was his friend
As one might guess
Aiden's room was a mess
Hands-on his mom' hip
And a stiff upper lip
"What happened to this room?"
Mom said, ready to fume.
Aiden started another one of his tales
He told of the green dragon with scales
Around the room, the dragon would fly
Knocking things off as he flew by
He'd land on the bed
Messing up the spread
His tail would sway
Swishing the toys every which way
After his tale, his mom would grin
And tell him to clean up his room again
To keep his room clean for a day,
She'd say, "You and your dragon go out and play."

Silly Sam

Silly Sam sang silly songs sleeping soundly.

Silly Sam snorted silly sounds sleeping soundly.

Silly Sam spoke silly syllables sleeping soundly.

Silly Sam snored silly sounds sleeping soundly.

Silly Sam stepped silly steps sleeping soundly.

Sleeping soundly, Silly Sam seemed silly.

Fun Without a Plan

Dilly Dally Who
What are we to do
Willy Wally Woe
Let's just go

Backward Bob

Backward Bob was a snob.

He lived in a backward mansion on the hill.

But this is a house no one would rob

If you went inside, you'd think it was unreal.

Family and guests must enter the back

The house staff must enter through the front door

He hung his coat on the shoe rack

Umbrellas must be left open on the floor

An oak dresser and mirror sit in the hall

With a tea kettle full of dead flowers

The floor and ceiling are switched throughout it all

The clock strikes 15 minutes past the hour

The front room is a sight to see

Pictures face the wall

The guest sits on a decorative toilet seat

On stands are kitchen pots standing tall

Nothing is as it should be

Everything is odd and strange

Oh, this house is a sight to see

Is he backward or deranged

Don't even ask where the staff work and roam

The butler is the cook

The Poolman cleans the home

The stableman takes your coat and puts it on a hook

The cat is the property Guard

While the dogs stay pinned in a cage

The horses run free in the yard

The bunnies have a temper and rage

At night, he wears flip-flops on his head

His clothes are turned around

He wears a tux to bed

He laughs when sleeping sound

When he drives proudly into town

Backward, his maid will drive

All his clothes are turned upside down

Down the street, he dances to a local dive

With hair in a purple blob

Orange and yellow clothes

How can backward Bob be such a snob

No one really knows.

Bedtime Tantrum

Fred turned red

Anger fed

When mom said

Go to bed.

Staying Quiet

Wiatt tried to be quiet.

He discovered life's a riot.

So, he decided to be defiant.

And laugh loud like a pirate.

Lou

Poor Lou

Got sick with the flu

With a runny nose, he blew and blew.

Many times, he sneezed, "Ha Choo!"

Several times vomit spew.

His mom knew what to do.

She called Dr. Sue.

Dr. Sue prescribed medicines to chew.

Mom made a brew of fish glue, goat rue, and a shoe.

Mom said, "We need to rub it all over you."

It cleared his nose as the smell oozed through.

It smelt like something that came from the zoo.

She made a nice chicken stew.

These things made the symptoms subdue.

Before long, Lou was like new.

But before he did, he was nice to pass it on to you.

Dylan

Dylan became a villain

He robbed banks for a million.

He joined with MacMillan

Soon, he had made a billion.

Bat

Ezra's up to bat
Swish and swat
Strike one goes the bat
Swish and swat
Strike two goes the bat
Swish and crack
Homerun goes the bat

Buster

Buster, my dog

Chased a frog.

He tripped over a tree

And somersaulted three.

Scared

Kelly got the

    Chilly Willy

        When scared by Milley.

Bawl Babies

Baby Billie blew bubbles by Brenda.

Baby Billie burped.

Brenda borrowed Bobby's bike.

Bobby babysat Baby Billy

Brenda bought Bananas.

Brenda bought Band-Aids

Baby Billie began bawling by Bobby.

Baby Billie bit Bobby.

Bobby bawled.

Brenda broke Bobby's bike.

Brenda, Baby Billie, and Bobby Bawled.

Sally

Prim and proper Sally

Went to the bowling alley.

She slipped on the floor

Making it the only strike she scores.

Poo

What do you do

When on the bottom of your shoe

Is doggie poo?

Legos

Legos are like life

They are fun to play

Until you don't put them away

Stepping on one causes pain and strife

Then you put them away for the rest of your life

Nature's Playground

"Communing with nature like planting, camping, rock climbing, hiking, kayak and playing in the rain .etc, teaches love and respect for the planet that provides us with food, water, air, and a thriving environment. But it also gives us a way to enjoy life through the crazy times, peace in the middle of chaos, and the ability to overcome challenges." – Deborah Ann Martin

My Best Friend

Llamas are my best friend.
It has become a trend.
With this gentle beast
We make yarn from their fleece.
They are so gentle and dear.
They get excited when I'm near.
They listen to me when I talk
They like it when we go for a walk
They don't mind carrying my sack
So I put it on their back
When I talk about my day
They listen and play.
I teach, and they learn.
For all this, they give me love in return

The Chase

A cat with a string

Puppy playing in the yard

Chasing his long tail

Right Is Never Easy

On a beautiful summer day,

Rabbit had his friends Fox and Lion over to play.

Rabbit's mom worked hard

Tending to the garden and yard

Fox took a broom

Started playing ball in the room

Lion said, very proud

"Playing ball in the house is not allowed."

Rabbit also wanted to have fun

So, he took the broom and ball for a run

Up went the ball

Mom's favorite vase took a fall

Fox said, "Hide it under the chair."

"No one will know it is there."

"Tell your mom," Lion said briefly

"Doing what is right is never what is easy."

"Put it behind that box,"

"Just deny what happened," said Fox.

Outside, it started to rain

Mom came in tired and drain

Rabbit looked a little bum

Because he knew the moment had come

In his mom, he should confide

Or take the vase and hide

He decided not to lie

He told his mom with a sigh

She made him work to pay for the vase

But then, after that, he lived happier days.

Brown Bear

When you see a Brown Bear

Do you get a scare

Jump in the air

Or act like you don't care?

Dog Days

On the soft couch lies

Undercover spies

Dog peak

Tempting to his eyes

After food, he tries

Dog sneak

For his owner cries

Until seen with eyes

Dog Speak

Fly, Butterfly, Fly

Fly, butterfly, fly.

Fly until you reach the sky.

Such grace you portray.

Softly, you flutter away.

Beautiful colors adorn your wings.

Wings of splendor and elegance of queens.

Fly, butterfly, fly.

Fly until you reach the sky.

Ape

Justin ate a banana

        And a grape

                Cause he's an ape.

Fawn

A baby fawn rests with

Her legs folded in a grass field.

The sun's warmth brings comfort

While the gentle wind strokes her fur.

The swaying wildflowers fragrant the air.

Her eyes slowly become heavy.

As the birds softly sing nearby.

Horse Race

My name is Chase

I win first place

When I horse race.

4 Kittens at Play

Mama is on the couch laying.

Her four kittens are in the room playing.

One is tangled in a ball of yarn.

One is pawing at an animal in a toy barn.

One is dipping his paw in a fishbowl.

One has a toy mouse he pats and rolls.

They're full of curiosity and energy each day.

The kittens rush for their milk without delay.

They drink their milk by lapping.

Tired, they go to mama to start napping.

Ducks

I saw ducks swimming today.

Did they splash and play?

How many?

Maze

Dog

    Chases cat

        Cat chases rat

            Rat solves the maze

The Laughing Owl

On a dark, gloomy night
The laughing owl takes flight.
His plumage of yellowish-brown stripes and a face of white
And eyes so big they give perfect sight.

At Blue Cliffs in Canterbury, he rarely achieved great heights.
His loud cry of dismal shrieks gives such a fright.
Chasing his prey on foot was his plight.
Beware of lizards, birds, rats, and mice, for the owl is out tonight.

He searches for food to bring to his mate that night.
On the rocky ledges, his dried grass nest sat out of sight.
There rests the female, who sits on the two white eggs all night.
The male returning with dinner brings such delight.

Twenty-five days later, the nest is no longer quiet, but little beaks are now in sight.

Anew

snow melts on the ground

sleeping flowers are awake

buds turn to green leaves

Dancing with Nature

On a warm summer day
Cassady danced away
On her toes and heals
She danced through flower fields

      With the birds, she'd sing
      Leaping as if she had wings
      She had beauty and grace
      As she pranced in place

She'd glide and twirl
Then gives a little whirl
In the summer heat
She was light on her feet

      As happy as can be
      Dancing, she felt so free
      Not a care in the world
      As she glided and Twirled

What she really loved
Was seeing the clouds dancing above
Nature played her song
As Cassady danced along.

Baby Frog

I was reading poetry

A baby frog jumped up to see

Staring at the words, did he

Then he hopped away gleefully.

Fluffy Clouds

As I lay

Under a palm tree,

I look at the fluffy clouds.

A big lion is staring at me.

I watch as the fluffy clouds.

Move over the sea

Under A Tree

Summer day spent under a tree.
There's no other place to be.
This is a relaxing place.
Summer's wind touches the face.

Gentle breezes touch the hair.
Fresh smell of nature is everywhere.
Squirrels jump from branch to branch.
Tree trunks crawling with little ants.

Birds merrily sing their songs.
Nature's active all day long.
Four busy bees buzz on by.
Butterflies caress the sky.

Little crickets chirp all day.
In the soft breeze, flowers sway.
There's no other place to be.
This is a relaxing place for me.

Sunset

Oh, how I would like to be

Walking along the shore

Picking up shells galore

As the sun meets the rolling sea.

Fall

Fall is my favorite season.

Here are a few of my reasons:

The air is crisp and sharp.

The wind whistles like a harp.

The leaves are pretty yellow, orange, red, and brown.

It's majestic to see them drift to the ground.

I love to hear the leaves crack under my feet.

Of all the holidays, Halloween is such a treat.

After Halloween follows Thanksgiving Day,

This is one of my favorite holidays.

It's a time of sharing with family and friends.

Thanksgiving means Christmas shopping begins.

People start to hustle and bustle about.

Sometimes, finding the perfect gift is hard to figure out.

Fall is the time for laughter and sharing.

Fall is full of holidays, decorations, and caring.

Playing in the Rain

‘ ‘ ‘ ‘ ‘ ‘ ‘ ‘ o ‘

‘ ‘

‘ ‘

‘ ‘ ‘ ‘ ‘ ‘ ‘ ‘ ‘ ‘ ‘ ‘ “ ‘

‘ ‘

‘ ‘ ‘ ‘ ‘ ‘ ‘ ‘ ‘ ‘ ‘ ‘ ‘ “ ‘

‘ ‘ ‘ ‘ Laney and Janie‘ ‘ “ ‘ “ ‘ ‘ “ ‘ ‘ “ ‘ ‘ ‘ “ ‘ ‘ “ ‘ ‘ ‘ “ ‘ ‘ “ ‘ ‘ “ ‘ ‘ ‘

‘ ‘ ‘ ‘ ‘ ‘ ‘ ‘ Acted zany‘ ‘ ‘ “ ‘ ‘ “ ‘ ‘ ‘ “ ‘ ‘ ‘ “ ‘ ‘ “ ‘ ‘ ‘ “ ‘ ‘ “ ‘ ‘

“ ‘ ‘ “ ‘ ‘ ‘ ‘ ‘ ‘ “ ‘ ‘ ‘ While playing in the rainy. ‘ ‘ “ ‘ ‘ “ ‘ ‘ “ ‘ ‘ “ ‘ ‘ ‘

‘ ‘ ‘ ‘ ‘ ‘ ‘ o ‘

‘ ‘

‘ ‘

‘ ‘ ‘ ‘ ‘ ‘ ‘ ‘ ‘ ‘ ‘ ‘ “ ‘

‘ ‘

‘ ‘ ‘ ‘ ‘ ‘ ‘ ‘ ‘ ‘ ‘ ‘ ‘ “ ‘

‘ ‘ ‘ ‘ ‘ ‘ ‘ ‘ ‘ ‘ ‘ ‘ ‘ “ ‘

‘ ‘ ‘ ‘ ‘ ‘ ‘ ‘ ‘ ‘ ‘ ‘ ‘ “ ‘

‘ ‘

‘ ‘ ‘ ‘ ‘ ‘ ‘ ‘ ‘ ‘ ‘ ‘ ‘ ‘ “ ‘

The Night Owl

On a dark, starry night

The owl takes flight.

What a perfect sight.

To see it out tonight

It gives such a delight

Just to catch sight.

The Giant

On a fall day

A spider crawled her way.

The itsy-bitsy spider

Looked like a giant beside her

She let out a shrill

And ran down the hill

The spider crawled away

Enjoying the fall day

Snow

Snow

Feels cold

On your nose

As it gently

Falls down from

Fluffy

Clouds

Circus Animal

Circus animals were the reason to go

They were the best part of the show

Unlike the circus animals of old

A new type has unfold

Horses prance

Bears dance

Dogs fly through the sky

Elephants rise high

Seals balance on balls

Monkeys juggle sticks

Lions do tricks

Bears ride tricycles

Clowns with cats ride motorcycles

Animal acrobats tumble

Tigers perform with a rumble

But now when you go

The animals are a hologram show

Dragonfly

On a rock stood a dragonfly

A long, sleek body

And four wings that fluttered in the wind.

His front legs scratched his head

Then, off he flies gracefully in the wind.

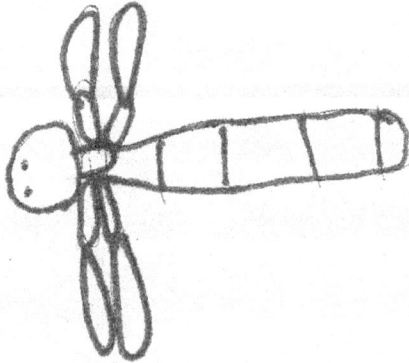

Robins

Robins in the sky

Souring up on high

Birds Rest

Eats worms from the ground

Robin chooses mate

Bird's Nest

Momma lays the eggs

Babies fly away

Bird's blessed

Zoo

Going to the zoo

Is my favorite thing to do.

How about you?

Is there any other way

Then to spend the whole day?

Hurling, Curling Snail

Sea or land, you slide through life

Strapped with a shell on your back

Slimy mucus left in your wake

Surface friction is reduced

So why are you still so slow

Sure, the shell might add extra weight

Snail-like slugs that have no shells are still slow. Why?

Sleeping Cat

Asleep with a snore

On the couch by the door

Cat Lays

Jumps high off the floor

Landing on all four

Cat Plays

Back to the place before

On the couch by the door

Cat Lays

Koala

A koala is as cute as can be
When it's holding onto a tree.
It loves eucalyptus leaves
Which makes it as slow as can be
In a pouch is the baby
That is called a Joey.

Cheetah

Cheetah kits wrestle and play

Tripping and tackling all day

Sometimes, tug of war, pouncing,

Or tripping to send the other bouncing

In the tall grass, they'll sneak and hide

Until they run by their mom's side

Seasons

new grass pokes through the rain-soaked ground.

fresh, lush, rich spring

grass dances in the wind.

plants, fields, beds, summer

green grass are the backdrop for wildflowers.

country, uncut, rough, fall

at morning light, animals graze in the pastures.

thin, changing plains, winter

grass peaks through the melting snow.

short meadows, slopes, seasons

Snow Friends

On two ends of the earth

Both penguins and Polar bears give birth

Penguins slide across the ice

Polar bears' skin is black, not white

Penguins stand over eggs they lay

Polar bears smell over a mile away

Both jump from great heights

Into the water and ice.

They love to swim all-day

So if together, they'd be friends and play.

Isabella

Isabella Marie

Sat under a tree

Watching a bee

Dance on flowers happily.

Buck

At morning's early light
I glimpsed a majestic sight
Sitting by the roaring falls
I could enjoy nature's all
The sun barely over the crest
Birds chirping in their nest
Brilliant colors lit the sky
Fluffy clouds scattered up high
I was in luck
Along the water was a buck
Oh what a sight to see
He looked majestic and free
As the wind made the flowers dance
Across the fields, it pranced
Stunning with its head held high
A graceful leap as it seemed to fly
As it stopped for a few moments to graze
I stood in awe and amaze
It could have been the rising sun I think
I thought it gave me a wink
No picture could capture this scene
So beautiful and serene

Squirrels

Squirrels play in flowers, bushes, and trees

They crack open nuts with sharp teeth

They eat nuts, fruit, and seeds

They carry them in a pouch in the cheek

They jump an amazing 15 feet

They can run at fast speeds

At the end of day, they sleep in trees

Circles

Cat chases a string

In the green grass of the yard

Dog chases its tail

Activities Of a Flower

There is beauty to behold

As the bud of a flower unfolds,

Dew on the petals glimmer in the sun.

The activities on the flower have just begun.

The bee is the first to come by.

He takes the nectar, and off he flies.

The butterfly stops to rest.

Then flutters off to the west.

An elderly lady stops to admire the petals.

A homeless person bends to take a smell.

The ants march this way and that way.

The wind makes it sway.

Finally, it's the end of the day.

A little boy takes the flower away.

He hands it to his mother with love.

She admires it and places it on the windowsill above.

Animals

A   Always great fun to watch

N   No petting without permission

I   In learning, we protect and care for them

M   Many animals are only seen at night

A   All have a purpose in the cycle of life

L   Love and respect all types of animals

S   Save the animals

Hippity Hoppity

Hippity, Hoppity, Ho

The bunny hops to and fro.

Hippity, Hoppity, Ho

Watch the bunny go.

Skunk

Soft with a tail fluffy and fat

Many think it looks like a cat

It eats fruit, grass, bugs and bees

It lives in hollow trees

It would be a great pet, I think

If you could remove the stink

Chickens

chickens are my favorite pet

i watch them hunt and peck

in the coop they dwelled

mine liked to be held

the rooster says, cock-a-doodle-doo

baby chicks are adorable too

when i come near the cage

they come to me and beg

to be pet or food

best is the new chicks when they brood

Farm Life

The sun shines bright in the sky

Floating through the air is a butterfly

Bouquet of wildflowers across the land

The farm animals are fed by hand

In the fields, horses run

The dogs play and have fun

Sheep and cows graze in the field

While farmers bring in their yield

Singing birds glide through the sky

While ducks quack in a pond nearby

Beautiful green and flowering trees

Sway in the gentle breeze.

Pets

No one loves animals more than Erin
She should have been a veterinarian
Erin takes care of them in her special way
Erin and the animals snuggle and play
She enjoys taking care of them, too
She's made her home a mini-zoo
Toys scatter the house
Her cats play with a toy mouse
Catwalks line the wall
The dogs chase a ball
She snuggles with the ferrets and bunnies
Watching her chickens play is funny
She holds the lizard and snake
Her fish follow her when she's awake
Erin has so much love to give each day
She shares it with her pets in so many ways
When she turns out the lights
It's time for them to settle in for the night.

Think, Learn, Rhyme!

"Everyone has something to teach, and everyone has something to learn. We can help each other by sharing what we know."- Deborah Parise

Class*

Bell ringing

Children sitting

Teachers educating

Grammar and Math learning

Science experimenting

History reviewing

Successful future

~Class~

Future successful

Reviewing History

Experimenting Science

Learning Math and Grammar

Educating Teachers

Sitting Children

Ringing Bell

*I wrote this poem is part of a poetry game with my son Chris.

Repairing 7 Days a Week

Christian is a mechanic who repairs different automobiles.

On <u>Monday</u>, he repaired a red Oldsmobile.

On <u>Tuesday</u>, he repaired a black Mazda.

On <u>Wednesday</u>, he repaired a green Honda.

On <u>Thursday</u>, he repaired a yellow Suzuki.

On <u>Friday</u>, he repaired a purple Mitsubishi.

On <u>Saturday</u>, he repaired his own blue Subaru.

On <u>Sunday</u>, he repaired his mother's white BMW.

Amanda's A To Z Presents

Amanda wanted to give a present to Dad.

She wanted to find something he had not had.

First, she went to the mall.

She saw APPLES and BALLS.

In the pet store, she saw CATS and DOGS.

She also saw EELS and FROGS.

She pictured her dad in a GO-CART or a HAND GLIDER.

She decided to buy Dad an ICE CREAM CONE.

It started to melt, so she licked it until it was gone.

Maybe she should get a JIGSAW or a KITE.

She could find the present that was just right.

She knew her dad already had a LAWNMOWER.

She did not know what to buy, so she asked her mother.

Her mother said that any present would be special.

Amanda saw the costume of a MARSHAL.

She thought about a hammer and NAILS.

There were OSTRICHES or PAILS.

Maybe the perfect present is a QUILT or a ROPE.

Amanda sat down and was about to give up hope.

She could get a SAILBOAT, a TOOL, an UMBRELLA, or a VINE.

There were so many things she couldn't make up her mind.

In the other stores, she saw a WATCH and a XYLOPHONE.

She could not find the perfect present, so she went home.

A YO-YO or even a ZEBRA might be the perfect present.

She could not find something she thought was decent.

Then she remembered what her mother said.

She climbed on Dad's lap and hugged and kissed him instead.

"I love you, dad!"

Dad said, "This is the best present I ever had."

Colors

PURPLE panda patted Penny's pig.

YELLOW yak yawned.

BLUE bear blew bubbles.

WHITE walrus went wading.

PINK penguin picked petunias.

GREEN gorilla grabbed grapes.

BLACK beaver bit bark busily.

RED reindeer raced Randy Rat.

BROWN bunny bounced balls.

Senses Poem

I See... <u>sunrise over the hills</u>. The sight is...<u>pretty</u>

I Hear...<u> bullfrog.</u> The sound is...<u> ribbit</u>

I Smell...<u> mom's cooking.</u> The smell is...<u> delicious</u>

I Touch...<u> slimy goo.</u> The feeling is...<u>gross</u>

I Taste...<u> fudge.</u> The taste is...<u> sweet.</u>

Playground Fun

Adele skipped around with Rochelle

Bree laughed with Marie

Clarence pretended to be in the army with Terrence

Darlene Jumped rope with Charlene

Eddie climbed monkey bars with Freddie

Faye Played hopscotch with Mae

Ginnie was talking with Winnie

Horace slid down the slide with Borace

Ivan pretended to be a knight with Marvin

Joan smiled at Sloan

Kendall spun around the merry-go-round with Wendell

Lawrence see-sawed with Florence

Matt swung higher than Pat

Nadine did flips with Pauline,

Olly climbed the monkey bars with Molly

Paul drew with chalk with Saul

Quinn bounced the ball to Gwyn

Ricky played basketball with Mickey

Sam played tag with Pam

Tori did penny drops off the bars with Morrie

Uri raced Cory

Velma talked in the tube with Thelma

Wylie played pretend with Miley

Xena spun the hula hoop with Lena

Zach played Capture the Flag with Mac

Monthly Play

In *January*, Alyssa tries to keep her resolutions day and night.

In *February*, Aaron makes Valentines red and white.

In *March*, Larry looks for his St. Patrick's Day gold.

In *April*, Brandon fools Justin with things he told.

In *May*, Marilynn enjoyed the flowers she was planting.

In *June*, Elizabeth has a pretend wedding.

In *July*, Michael watches fireworks at night.

In *August*, John swims while it's still light.

In *September*, Joshua enjoys no school on Labor Day.

In *October*, Tabatha finds a costume for a play.

In *November*, Josiah helps prepare for Thanksgiving Festivities.

In *December*, Eddie is happy with all the Christmas Activities.

Four Seasons

Spring is the flowers after the rain.
It's the children planting gardens.
Spring is the birds hatching from an egg.
It's waiting for school buses.

Summer is the warmth of the sun on high.
It's the children swimming and picnicking.
Summer is the baby birds taking flight.
It's the end of another school year.

Fall is the leaves falling in the wind.
It's the children singing on hayrides.
Fall is the bird fully grown.
It's the beginning of school days.

Winter is the snowflakes glistening in the sky.
It's the children sledding downhill.
Winter is the bird that migrated away.
It's the school's holiday break.

Austin's Opposites

Austin's mommy took him out to play.

He had the opposite kind of day.

In the **beginning**, he went to the playground.

At the **end** of his day, he had to lie down.

Austin climbed **up** the slide.

Then he slid **down** the slide.

He played on the **small** chin-up bar.

He played on the **tall** chin-up bar.

He went **up** on the see-saw.

He went **down** on the see-saw.

Austin was **near** his mommy on the merry-go-round.

Austin was **far** from his mommy on the merry-go-round.

He went **over** to the jungle gym.

He went **under** the jungle gym.

In the sandbox, he **filled** his bucket.

In the sandbox, he **emptied** his bucket.

He walked on the **short** balance bar.

He walked on the **long** balance bar.

He came to the **front** of the swing.

He went to the **back** on the swing.

Austin was **happy** playing.

Then Austin became **sad**.

He was **dry,** but it began to rain.

Now, he was **wet.**

His mommy said he could no longer be **out.**

Now he had to go **in.**

Who Are You, Letter U

Are you half full or half empty?

Are your insides hot or cold?

D

R

I

N

K

Are you plain or fancy?

Are you delicate or sturdy?

Sounds Of Life

Achoo sneezed the policeman with allergies

Baa said the sheep on the way to the barn

Cock-a-doodle-doo, the rooster shouted in the morning

Ding dong went the doorbell

Eek! screamed the lady who saw a mouse

Fizz went the red soda in the glass

Gobble gobble, said the fat turkey

Ha-ha laughed the kid after telling a joke

Ick said the little girl who stepped on gum

Jingle Jingle of the change in the boy's pocket

Knock Knock was the sound on the door

Lap lap went the kitten who drank milk

Moo said the black cow

Neigh when the horse after trotting

Oink said the pig in the pen

Pitter-patter went the rain as it hit the roof

Quack quack said the yellow duck

Ring went the cell phone

Screech said the passing owl

Tick tock, the clock struck one

Ugh is a teen's reply to chores

Vroom goes the sports car

Whoosh, the basketball made the basket

Yawn went tired, mom

Zoom went the dad in his fast car

I Can't Write a Poem

Forget it

You must be kidding

Don't have the time

Can't think of a theme

Would rather watch TV

Would rather do anything else

I can't think of anything

I can't figure out a rhyme

I don't feel like it

My head is full of other stuff

Times Up? Uh Oh!

All I have is a dumb list of excuses

Do you like it? Really. No kidding.

Thanks a lot, would you like another?

Be

Changes start with me.
If I want to be the
Best that I can be,
I need to work on the BEs.
Others may not agree
But I am doing this for me.

Be courteous
Be considerate
Be cooperative
Be kind
Be friendly
Be responsible
Be polite
Be nice
Be helpful
Be respectful
Be thoughtful

A Fare for The Fair

Michelle, Tiffany, and Linda paid a **fare** to attend the **fair**.

Tiffany entered a **pair** of strawberry-**pear** pies.

She **won** a prize for **one** of her pies.

So she could enter another contest; she had to **sew** two items.

Tiffany was called **to** the winner's circle for the **two** entries.

Michelle told Tiffany **"bye"** as she went **by** the freak shows.

She saw a **hare** with purple **hair**.

She saw a **bear** that was **bare** except for the hair on his head.

"Oh, **Dear**," she exclaimed as she saw three antlers on a **deer**.

Michelle saw a wind **vane** shaped like a monster with red **veins**.

Linda went to **their** favorite spot, where **there** were shows and games.

She saw **acts** of men juggling an **axe**.

She found her **way** to the game, where they guess how much you **weigh**.

Next, she **threw** a ball **through** a hoop and won.

She watched a show about a man who **slay** a monster in a **sleigh**.

Under the heat of the **sun**, the girls saw Annie's **son**.

All they could do was **stare** as they saw him on those **stairs**.

Tiffany ran to **him** and asked to sew the **hem** of his pants.

Linda **blew** kisses as she sashayed to his side in her **blue** dress.

This made Michelle as **ill** as an **eel** out of water.

Michelle refused to act like a piece of **meat** as she went to **meet** him.

The **four** walked around the fair **for** a few hours.

They went **here** and there to **hear** different concerts.

They saw on a grate a "**no** entry" on a sign and wanted to **know** why.

They didn't know what to **do due** to the situation.

They thought it might be **great** to go through the **grate**.

In the area, they saw a **principal** shouting their **principles**.

He was so crazy he was drinking **tea** and spitting out a golf **tee**.

He stood by his pet **yew**, Then shouted, "Hey **you**!!!!"

Scared the **four** ran **for** the gate hoping not to get into trouble.

Writing Poems

Emily had to write poems for school
She didn't think it was cool
She wasn't sure how to rhyme
Now, she needed to do it all the time
She started a new trend
She asked something from all her friends
"Let's pass our notes with a rhyme"
Eventually, it became fun in time
In the class all year, they received an A
Rhyming became a fun new way

Counting on Fun

One kid likes to have fun

Two kids like to ride in a canoe

Three kids like to climb a tree

Four kids like to swim ashore

Five kids like swim and dive

Six kids like to sword fight with sticks

Seven kids like to eat cake that tastes like heaven

Eight kids like to roller-skate

Nine kids like to sit under a tree and recline

Ten kids like to play with a friend

Name ABC's

Amy ate apples.

Bob bit Bananas.

Carl can cook.

Dan dug ditches.

Eve enjoyed eggs.

Fred found frogs.

George got goats.

Harry had help.

Irene is insane.

Jack jumped jets.

Ken kissed Katie.

Larry loved Laura.

Mark met Maggie.

Nathan needed nails

.

O'Brien owned opals.

Paula picked petunias.

Quenton quoted queens.

Ron rode rollerblades.

Sam sang songs.

Tom typed t's.

Ulysses unfolded undershirts.

Vicky viewed videos.

Wayne wore whistles.

Xena x-rayed xylophones.

Zed zipped zippers.

Cody's Day at The Beach

Cody went to bed early at **night**.

He woke to the **morning** light.

"It is a pretty day to **play**."

"I'll wait to **work** another day."

Cody sat down on the **hot** beach.

He had a **cold** drink and a peach.

Cody sat **down** with lotion to apply.

He looked **up** to see the sky.

"What is the use of staying **dry** all day?"

"I've come to the beach to get **wet** today."

Cody swam **out** very far in the sea.

Then he came **in** as fast as can be.

Cody swam **above** the water.

Then he swam **under** water.

Cody built **up** castles in the sand.

He tore them **down** with his hand.

Cody was getting tired of **play**.

It was time to get some **work** done today.

Cody knew he had to **go**.

But he could **come** again, you know.

Red

Red is apples, crayons, and cars.

Red is the taste of spicy.

Red smells like playdough and cinnamon.

Red makes me feel angry and hot.

Red sounds yelling, honking in traffic jams, and chaotic music.

Red is a rose, strawberries, and a stop sign.

Red is wrong.

Red is canceled.

Red is wrong.

Red is a scorching hot summer day.

Adventure Grab Bag

"Success is not final, failure is not fatal: it is the courage to continue that counts." - Winston Churchill

Basketball Teamwork

Starting whistle blows
Who's gonna win no one knows
Carson loves this sport
He feels at home on the court
With his team, he works well
The way they move you can tell
The dribbling ball
Sets the rhythm for them all
Partnered with the opposing team
The dance is harder than it seems
Pass, dribble, dribble, pivots and turn
Dribble, dribble, the pass is returned
Fancy footwork across the floor
Fans shout and roar
Dribble, Dribble, Throws
Dribble, dribble, off it goes
Thunk, now it's a rebound
Someone swats it down
Partners glide across the floor
Dribble, Dribble some more
As time comes to a draw
Carson gets the ball
He is nimble and quick
His footwork is slick
Minutes until the end
A jump shot to swish it in
He made the final score
For a win, the crowd began to roar
Basketball is always fun
Especially when his team won.

Pillow

Pillow

      Soft, fluffy

            Comfort

If I Could Choose My Name

If I could choose my name,

Would I choose one from a season:

Like Summer, Spring, or Winter.

If I could choose my name,

Would I choose one from scripture:

Like Grace, Faith, Hope, or Charity.

If I could choose my name,

Would I choose one from a place:

Like Phoenix, Dallas, or India.

If I could choose my name,

Would I choose one from songs music:

Like Amanda, Eileen, Beth, or Amy.

If I could choose my name,

Would I choose one that is unique:

Like Childuberry, Tacaree, or Ashawnte.

If I could choose my name,

Would I choose one that is common:

Like Chad, Ralph, Jack, and Diane.

If I could choose my name,

Would I choose a different name?

Nah, my name was specially picked for me.

Cookie Jar

I wanted a cookie from the cookie Jar.

I saw it on the counter from afar.

To me, the cookies did not belong.

Just taking one would be wrong.

So, I decided to do what was right.

I asked Mom if I could have one tonight.

Race

The girl ran at the track meet.

Did she run fast too?

Win the race?

Hole

I stepped into a small hole.

How was the hole made?

What's in it?

Kyle's Travels

Kyle wanted to travel far.

He started driving a car.

He ran out of gas.

Kyle wanted to travel fast.

He rode on a plane.

He couldn't see the terrain.

Kyle wanted to travel to the stars.

His mother said a rocket would take him too far.

So he wasn't able to go.

Kyle wanted to travel to a show.

He thought he'd like to ride an elephant.

But he didn't know how to make an elephant prance.

Kyle wanted to travel to a faraway land.

He thought he'd ride a buggy on the sand.

He discovered there were too many hot days.

Kyle wanted to travel in so many ways.

He decided the library gave him a way to explore.

He opened a book and traveled forevermore.

Roses Are Red

Roses are Red
Violets are blue
I wrote this as a kid
How about you?

Dress Up

Kendall was a beautiful queen

With a tiara and ballroom dress in green

Standing by the mirror, she stood

Kendall is Little Red Riding Hood.

Dressed as a ballerina, angel, fairy, and rocker in cleats

A puckered lip to look charming and sweet

Tomorrow, the dress will be a Zombie, devil, pirate, or witch

No more beauty; it's time for an evil switch.

A puppy who gives a yelp

A superhero, doctor, or nurse who can help.

Adventure can be found in a whirl

As Kendall changes into an Indian or cowgirl.

From the rising of the sun,

Kendall's day has begun.

Whatever her fantasy,

That is what Kendall will be.

Nana

Hannah and Ana

Went to see Nana

Who lives in Montana?

Sweet and Loving

Evie is the sweetest little child
Being with her is so worthwhile
She is so full of love
She is definitely a gift from above.

It's fun to watch her laugh and play
Then gives hugs and kisses all day.
Despite the crazy strife
She is so full of life

Next to Papaw's giant dog, she's small
But it doesn't matter to her at all
She sneaks him food, pets him, and hugs him all day
Sometimes, they will even play

She's such an angel when she crawls on your lap.
She snuggles against you and takes a nap.

Warrior

Sean, great and mighty warrior, is he

Who sits on the throne of destiny

His faith, love, honor, and staying true

This will help guide his people through

A new adventure will begin

Evil in the village will end

Wisdom to make his people great

This was his fate.

Kayaking

With his family or alone
On the water, Colton's at home.
Sometimes his dog is a rider
As the kayak slips thru water sliders

The sun kissed lake gives a glimmering glow
As fish race down below
Sometimes they jump in the air
With their artistic flare.

As the hot air begins to squeeze
Along comes a gentle breeze
With a paddle with two sides
Thru the water he continues to glide

Beautiful birds sing in the tree
Out here, he feels so free.
He spots animals along the water's side
While thru the air a falcon glides

Nature seems to bless
When getting away from life's mess
As the sun begins to set
Leaving is always Colton's regret.

How To Get Peace

Toddler

Warm bathwater

Play with bath toys

Clean hair

Clean Body

Toweled

Warm Pajamas

Warm bed

Tucked In

Bedtime Prayers

Bedtime Stories

Blank Stare

Peace

Mountain House

                              t

                    n   a

                    u   i

          p   o   n

Went U   A   m   and

Crossed over a river ^^^^^^^^

To visit a friend. One winter visit. ""

The snow came down ' ' ' ' ' ' ' ' ' ' '

' ' ' ' ' ' ' ' ' ' ' it came down harder."""""

""

""

""

_____*the river FROZE*_____

I tried to leave and

S

  L

    I

     D

        D

        O

        W

        N

The

  t

  n   a

 u   i

 o   n

m   !!!!!!!!!!!!!!

What an Exciting and Scary Ride!!!

I didn't have to pay to ski or go on a r^o^l^l^e^r Coaster

Noble Knight

Sir Maverick, a Noble Knight

Was good and right

Showed all the light

So he never had to fight.

Pretend

Brian and Ryan played pretend

Brian was a lion lyin' in mount zion

Ryan was a Hawaiian

They played airplanes flyin'

Army men dyin'

They laughed so hard they were cryin'

Choice

Wayne doesn't like to be plain

In Bright colors, he dressed again and again.

Nancy doesn't like to be fancy

In jeans, she'd wear dancing

Jennifer doesn't like winter fur

In wool, she would prefer

Cary doesn't want to dress scary

In a formal, she dressed like Princess Aerie

Sammie doesn't like Cami

In the night, she prefers jammies

Bert doesn't like kilts or skirts

Instead, he prefers jeans and a T-shirt

Storm doesn't want to be in uniform

In all his dress, he goes against the norm

Gale doesn't like a wedding veil

At her wedding, her bun had Chinese decretive nails.

Frank doesn't like to look rank

In the latest styles, he always looks swank

Bie doesn't like wearing a tie

In his formal, he's not like the other guy

Nicky doesn't like clothes that are clingy or sticky

In all her clothes, she's very picky

Geraldine doesn't like to wear gabardines

Her favorite clothes are always jeans

Dora doesn't like to wear Fedora

In the winter, she loves her angora

Brock doesn't like his work smock

In the breakroom, he shows off his weird socks

Blair doesn't like anything with a flare

In her house, she wears just her underwear

Camile doesn't like chenille

In all settings, she has to have on heels

Bernice doesn't wear a chemise

In the evening, she wears her fleece

Family

Child

Parents

Grandparents

Aunts and Uncles

Cousin

Bump

Woe Ned

        Don't go to bed

                With a bump on your head

Shirley

Shirley woke early

Combs hair that's curly

Jewelry that's Pearlie

Dress that is girlie

Spins around whirling

Playing With Your Food

Kickball with potatoes
Curling with fries
Stickball with tomatoes
Hurling with pies
Laying with fruit
Eat on the run
Playing with your food
Neat and fun
Sliding with dips
Throwing with eggs
Riding with chips
Rowing with chicken legs
Knotting with spam
Swaying with beef stewed
Nothing is better than
Playing with your food

Fall Festivals

Exciting events come in fall.

Fall festivals enjoyed by all.

There's so much fun under the sun.

Fall festivals are so much fun.

Cotton Candy, hotdogs, and more.

So much food you'd want to explore.

There are so many games to be won.

Fall festivals are so much fun.

Hayrides, ponies, and a petting zoo.

Wow, there is so much you can do!

It is sad when the night is done.

Fall festivals are so much fun.

Things I Like Poem

Chocolate, God,

computers, cake,

kittens, puppies,

music, steak.

Four Seasons, nature,

flying, going for a hike,

These are all the

things I like.

Family, adventures,

friends, cook,

knowledge, swimming,

bubbling brook

things I like.

Festivals, movies,

fairs, waterfalls,

Touring, nature,

talking, biking,

These are all the

laugh, love,

animal calls,

Helping, sunrise,

holidays, motorbike,

These are all the

things I like.

What do you like?

Carousel Ride

Carousel Ride

Music and laughter draw you in.

Carousel Ride

The kid in you will go inside.

The blue-painted pony will win.

The music and ride soon begin.

Carousel Ride

Halloween

Halloween is a fun time of the year.

kids dressing as their favorite

characters. Adults dressing up

and decorating up

their homes. All for the

exchange of the

delicious

candy

treats.

Fishing Trip

The sun was starting to rise

It was an early start for Elias

He loaded his boat the size of a tub

He loaded his tackle, bait, and pole

He headed off to Camp Drake

Acres of water that is just three feet deep

He put his boat and gear into the lake

He whistled as he took his boat out

Elias raced as fast as lightning

Beating another fisherman to his favorite site

Relaxing and Casting

A nibble and a bite

A jerk and a tug

His pole began to bend

Feeling confident and smug

He tried to bring in the fish

This seemed to be a big one

Letting go might be a mistake

Feet firmly locked into the boat bow

The boat was pulled around the lake

Thud, bang, crash

The boat hit a log in the water

Elias flew out of the boat with a splash

Pole still in hand

He stood to his feet

He was so angry steam came out of both ear

Flames shot from his head

He reeled and brought the fish near

He grabbed the four-foot fish

Threw it to the shore

He fried it up and put it in a dish

He was determined to eat it all

He had won this battle

Elias gave a big grin

Sat under a shade tree

Pondering when the next round would begin.

Foot

Foot

stinky,

sore, dirty

flat, bare, slender

webbed

Hobgoblin

Chris was a Hobbledehoy.

He saw a rambunctious hobgoblin.

Cattywampus from him.

It gave him the collywobbles.

He drew his snickersnee from its sheath

Cutting the air widdershins.

Chris gave the warning cry, 'Gardyloo!'

The hobgoblin seemed bumfuzzled.

He began striking the hobgoblin's bulbous back

Exposing gubbins in the perturbing bulbs

Chris felt borborygm as he looked at the hobgoblin

The hobgoblin laughed as he sialoquent

He was a slangwhanger who used Billingsgate

" You silly nincompoop, I am an old fuddy-duddy.

Do you think I am going to mollycoddle you?

I am a frugivore. As you go down my throat,

I am sure you'll cause some Crapulence.

But it will be Comeuppance for your Fatuous,"

Chris was a namby-pamby that refused to Lollygag

He ran Lickety-split for a vomitory

The hobgoblin laughed his head off

Because he was a pettifogger

With being a troglodyte, getting into

Shenanigans was his only entertainment

Fearless

Dan and John Coast

They are the most

Fearless, they'd boast

Until they saw a ghost

Now, both are behind a bedpost

Summer Camp

Horseback riding, sliding

Kickball, stickball

Cheering, mountaineering

Tag, capture the flag

Lacrosse, ring toss

Crafting, rafting

Race, chase

Ring, swing

Hiking, biking

Bows, rows

Crewing, canoeing

Ropes, water Floats

Balloon toss, toss across

Throwing, rowing

Track, hacky sack

Game In

raiden loves game in

the enemies he'll keep defeat in

until they're wore in down

once they are beat in

he's win in

finally he's the champ in

Grandmother

Grandmother

Loving, nurturing, caring

Happy!

Swim Meet

Standing on the platform,

Rhiana knows some of

The other swimmers.

She's talked with them.

She's swam against them before

Smiles and nods are exchanged

In position

As the buzzer sounds,

Rhiana and the other swimmers dive into the cool, crisp water

Like ballerinas, they gracefully swim to the top

Each stroke and breath methodically took

A race to beat her own time

A race to win that heat

A race for her team to win the competition

As she reaches her flip turn,

Her body moves poetically as she practiced

Over and over again

One lap, two laps, three laps

There is no time for tiredness, aching, or burning

No time for mistakes

There is no time to see where the others are

However, in her peripheral vision, the swimmer next to her

She seems a little ahead

As the finish line approaches

More kick, more power in the arms, more determination

Hands cutting through the water

Her body moving like a well-tuned machine

The edge of that pool is the only thing on her mind

Two-hand touch on the side of the pool

No disqualifications

Buzzer sounds to end the heat

She won this heat

As she shakes the swimmers' hands

She knows some of these swimmers

Will be her biggest completion in other heats

For her team and herself, she must repeat

Her actions in the following heats.

Sneak For a Movie Geek

Alex, the movie geek

To see Star Wars, he did sneak

Caught by the movie Crew

Embarrassment like he never knew

Out the door, he did go

Never again snuck in a movie show

Cornfields

In the mind of a child

A cornfield is a magical place.

It's an enchanted forest,

A place to explore,

Or a place to find animals and bugs.

It's cover for a game of hide-in-seek.

Clearings where corn didn't grow

Becomes a house for a pretend family

Or a prison for Capture the Flag.

Nothing beats a cornfield for a game of tag.

The straight rows make lanes for a race.

It adds excitement as a maze.

As night falls, the field begins to change.

It's a game of tag with flashlights.

The clearing makes a perfect campsite.

The night animals come out.

It's such a fright.

To run through the cornfields at night

Day or night, the cornfield feeds a child's imagination.

My Daughter

My daughter is precious indeed.

She brings out the joy in me.

She looks precious in her Sunday dress.

She makes me laugh when her face is a mess.

She loves playing with her dolls.

She loves shopping at the malls.

She loves her special cat.

She loves playing dress-up with big clothes and hats.

She is determined to go her way.

Her spirit adds something special to each of my days.

My love for her will not falter.

For she is my darling little daughter.

Race

Reid loves to speed

        He stays in the lead

                Until winning's achieved.

Time with Dad

Hat, jeans, and boots
Tegan wakes her dad with "Hoots."
When saddling the horses, dad gave a yawn
Then, set off at the break of dawn.

She couldn't wait to see
Rivers, flowers, and birds in the tree
A picnic on the ground
With no one else around

Stopping to set camp at mid-day
They'd fish, hike, and play.
Later, they'll go through their sacks.
To prepare their dinner and snacks.

By the fire, her dad would sing a song
She'll laugh and sing along
Smores made by the fire
Next, it'll be time to retire

Take down the camp in the morning light
Riding back will be a delight
Spending this time with dad
Will be the best she ever had

Junk Or Treasure

As a girl, I had collections.

My reflections

Of special days

Or of neat things that caught my gaze.

In my room was the attic door

With a small floor.

A hiding place

For my treasures in the red case

My case had toys, paper, knick-knacks,

Old set of jacks,

Stuff, words of truth,

Pictures and cards of Rose and Ruth.

Our home sold; the case left behind.

Treasures to find.

Will the owners

Find value or feel it's junk.

Trouble

Children playing

Are usually laughing and loud.

When they're quiet,

Trouble can be found.

My Son

My son is a special little boy.

Like most, he has his favorite little toy.

His is a cute little teddy bear.

At night, he feels it protects him there.

He loves a good book.

He reads of Huck, Sawyer, and Captain Hook.

He digs in the dirt and looks for spiders and bugs.

He loves being friendly and gives kisses and hugs.

He is kind and good.

He tries hard to do what he should.

I thank God up above.

He gave me this precious son to love.

Captain Fin

Where do I begin
To tell about Fin
He was a captain
Who would go sailin'

Adventure's there'd be
Traveling the seas
The world he would see
While monsters would flee

Making evil right
He'd fight day and night
Pirates, he would fight
And laugh with delight

Stories to be told
Of Treasures and gold,
Mermaids, young and old,
Trolls ugly and bold,

Giant bees that sting
Monsters with giant wings,
Castles, queens, and king,
Dragons and other things,

Captain Fin and crew
Sailed the ocean-blue
Each quest they'd bid ado
What Next? No one knew.

Great Pappy

Her story was about to begin
The moment Audrey picked up the pen
A story about her great pappy
On adventures that made them happy
Her love for him would unfold
In each story that she told
Drawing and Coloring what's outside
Sharing it all with her great pappy with pride
She loved to sing to him all-day
He watched while she would play
Outside, she'd dance and climb
She and Pappy loved their special time
She'd help him along the way
And hate when it was the end of the day
As she was about to go
A special kiss she would always blow.

Football Legacy

Conner is a third-generation football player and fan.

Whether in the field or in the stands,

Football is part of their mind, body, and soul.

Nothing matters but their teams making a goal.

There's a connection between papaw, father, and son.

Whether being a player or a coach, the legacy is carried on.

The love for the game cannot be denied.

Pride is seen in his papaw's and his father's eyes.

You could see the pride beam

When Conner made running back for his team.

He has to receive a handoff to rush the ball.

He has to line up to catch it and not let it fall.

He helps block in some of the plays.

Other times, he throws when someone's in the way.

Football is serious, but it's also fun.

What he loves best is when he gets to run.

He grabs the ball and tucks it in.

Then takes off down the field for a win.

Sometimes, he's at the bottom of the pile.

But Conner holds onto the ball with style.

No one could believe their eyes.

When he still has the ball, they are mesmerized.

He's fast, agile, and has a sense of intuition that is strong

Running down the field is where he belongs.

When he runs and adds to the success of the team,

There's nothing more thrilling than the crowds' scream

Conner has a love for the game.

As he gets older, will he feel the same?

Will he continue to play

Will he be a coach one day

Will the legacy continue on

When he has a daughter or son.

Purple World

Glenda loves purple everything

She wears purple bling

She has purple hair

Purple's in all the clothes she wears

She wears purple shoes

Purple in anything she buys new

Her room has purple everywhere

She has a purple chair

She has a purple suitcase under the bed

On top is a purple pillow and spread

Purple is the color she'll always choose

If offered another she'll refuse

This purple world is so much fun

That's why Glenda makes it a special one.

Outside

we would play

outside all day

'til the time of night

when on came the street light.

Camping

Camping all-day
Launa loves to play
She sits by the water to watch the fish
On dandelions, she makes a wish
Birds fly high
Against the blue sky
Flowers move in the wind
Frogs jump again and again
When walking along a trail
She sees animals. It never fails.
As day turns to dusk
Starting a campfire is a must
Hot dogs and smores
Snacky foods galore
At night, the moon is so full and bright
Lightning bugs sparkle the night
Launa loves to watch the stars
Even though they seem so far
She watches their little lights
Twinkle in the night
Sometimes, they streak the sky
While a fluttering owl flies high
The sun rises, and she's awake
She Kayaks on the lake
Launa loves to play
 While camping another day

Barbie

Barbies
Everyone plays
In different ways
Talia's has pretty long hair
Malia's is short with a flair
Talia's dresses in pretty dresses
Malia's gets dirty and creates messes
Talia's drives a Barbie sports car
Malia's drives in a Tonka truck that goes far
Talia's has furniture bought for the Barbie Mansion
Malia's has homemade and in the middle of expansion
Talia's hangs with those who follow the trends
Malia's has action figures for her friends
Talia's man is Ken which everyone knows
Malia's man is the scruffy GI Joe
Talia's wears high heel shoes
Malia's wears boots that's blue
In different ways
Everyone plays
Barbies

Learning

Failure is just a learning opportunity
That will provide for a teaching opportunity
When success is finally found.

Index of Titles

"Children are the world's most valuable resource and it's best hope for the future" - John F. Kennedy

4

A

B

C

About the Author

Deborah Ann Martin is a poet and blogger at www.survivinglifelessons.com. She is a single mom of four adult children and has four grandchildren. She has been writing poetry for as long as she can remember. Deborah gains her inspiration from the crazy events of her life and the life she observes around her. She earned her MBA during her unique career path. She is a veteran and is currently working as a Computer Application Administrator. Her distinctive work and life have given her the knowledge and inspiration to write. This book is the first in a series.

In 2020, she was diagnosed with a rare cancer called uLMS. She calls it "fibroid-gone-bad". Since then, she started her website and started putting her poems into poem books. She has several children's books and other books in this Life Moment's Series. She has her books in English and Spanish.

About the Illustrator

Deborah Ann Martin has four grandchildren Ages 4-11. They have each done atleast one picture to place in this special book. This has been a great project for all of them. Since the pictures were going to be black and white, they did only pictures with outlines. She hopes that this will inspire them to accomplish their dreams. Deborah loved that they used their creativity to bring their interpretation of the poems to life.

Her grandchildren, love doing activities indoors and outdoors. They go to museums, zoos, play sports, active in school, kayaking, hiking and more. They also enjoy playing video games together.

www.ingramcontent.com/pod-product-compliance
Lightning Source LLC
Chambersburg PA
CBHW071125280326
41935CB00010B/1115